KU-130-524

# Poems from the Second World War

*Other books about war from Macmillan Children's Books*

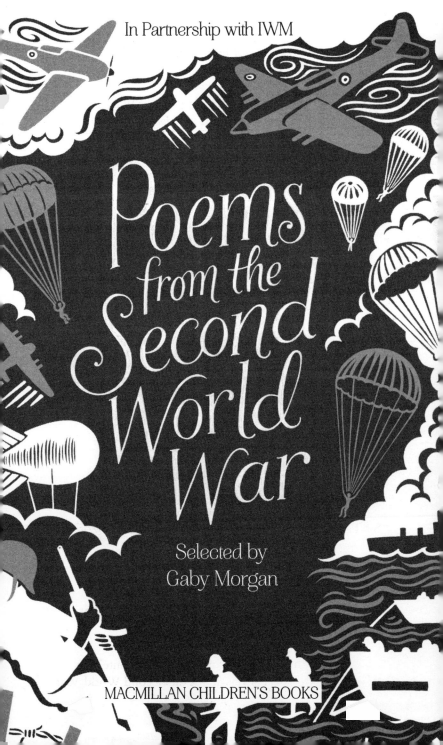

In Partnership with IWM

# Poems
## from the
## Second
## World
## War

Selected by
Gaby Morgan

MACMILLAN CHILDREN'S BOOKS

First published 2015 by Macmillan Children's Books
an imprint of Pan Macmillan
a division of Macmillan Publishers Limited
20 New Wharf Road, London N1 9RR
Associated companies throughout the world
www.panmacmillan.com

ISBN 978-1-4472-8499-4

iwm.org.uk

# CONTENTS

# Polliciti Meliora

As one who, gazing at a vista
    Of beauty, sees the clouds close in,
And turns his back in sorrow, hearing
    The thunderclouds begin.
So we, whose life was all before us,
    Our hearts with sunlight filled,
Left in the hills our books and flowers,
    Descended, and were killed.
Write on the stones no words of sadness –
    Only the gladness due,
That we, who asked the most of living,
    Knew how to give it too.

*Frank Thompson*

## SEPTEMBER, 1939

The purple asters lift their heads
Beneath the azure autumn skies;
Above the sunflower's golden cup
Hover the scarlet butterflies.

Not in the sandbagged city street
Where London's silver guardians soar,
But through the cottage garden throbs
The aching grief of England's war.

*Vera Brittain*

# In September 1939

The last war was my favourite picture story.
*Illustrated London News* bound in the study;
The German bayonet we believed still bloody

But was just rusty. Privacy of death.
My uncle's uniform meant more than glory;
Surprise that grief should be so transitory . . .

All the predictions of adolescence had
Disposed of glory in their realist path:
There'd be no need to duck and hold your breath.

Now, looking as useless and as beautiful
As dragonflies, the plump silver balloons
Hang over London also like zany moons.

Yet from the blacked-out window death still seems
Private, not an affair that's shared by all
The distant people, the flats, the Town Hall.

But some remember Spain and the black spots
They shouted 'Bombers' at. That memory screams
That we know as a film or in bad dreams.

Fear will alight on each like a dunce's cap
Or an unguesscd disease unless death drops
Quicker than the sirens or the traffic stops.

*Bernard Gutteridge*

# Bournemouth, September 3rd, 1939

My summer ends, and term begins next week.
Why am I here in Bournemouth, with my aunt
And 'Uncle Bill', who something tells me can't
Be really my uncle? People speak
In hushed, excited tones. Down on the beach
An aeroplane comes in low over the sea
And there's a scattering as people reach
For towels and picnic gear and books, and flee
Towards the esplanade. Back at the hotel
We hear what the Prime Minister has said.
'So it's begun.' 'Yes, it was bound to.' 'Well,
Give it till Christmas.' Later, tucked in bed,
I hear the safe sea roll and wipe away
The castles I had built in sand that day.

*Anthony Thwaite*

# THE SECOND WORLD WAR

The voice said 'We are at War'
And I was afraid, for I did not know what this
    meant.
My sister and I ran to our friends next door
As if they could help. History was lessons learnt
        With ancient dates, but here

Was something utterly new,
The radio, called the wireless then, had said
That the country would have to be brave. There
    was much to do.
And I remember that night as I lay in bed
        I thought of soldiers who

Had stood on our nursery floor
Holding guns, on guard and stiff. But war meant
    blood
Shed over battlefields, Cavalry galloping. War
On that September Sunday made us feel frightened
        Of what our world waited for.

*Elizabeth Jennings*

# Newgale Sands 1940

Every Year
There is a short season
When the summer buses from the market town
Routed to the farthest rock of western Wales
Stop where the road swoops down upon the shore
At Newgale Sands:
The wind-rutted bungalows
Taking their crazy shutters down
Hoist the gay semaphores
The signal summer,
The sun blares in through doors
Blistering on sandy hinges,
Down in the bay
The rocks stare motionless
Into the August mirror of the sea.

But in June
When the honey honeysuckle is thickest on the
   bush
The wind blows off the sea
And no one comes,
In any year
No season has begun then.
Only this year we know it never will begin,
None will come but those
Like us, to say goodbye, sisters to brothers,
Lovers to lovers.

This quite deserted year
We saw Newgale sands as men
Shipwrecked see the waiting island,
Two miles of bay still wet
At midday from the morning tide
Under the thick English summer sky
Which only lets the warmth through not the sun;
There was a noon tide bearing on the land
The unremitting roar
Of endless breakers racing
With furious hair after the fretted surf

Scattered like whitened bones on the flat sand;
And here, entangling the noon light,
A fresh stream glancing
Ice-cold out of the generous rock
For those thirsty and ragged landing

From the sun-baked boats,
And then the caves
Shelter for fires of driftwood
Within the echo, like a thousand underground falls,
Of never-quietened waves;
Limpets on the rocks, and warm pools streaming
With drowning weed, hiding crabs and crayfish,
Razor shells for knives,
And at last the green land, the turf
Growing to the cliff edge
Promising cornfields, promising sheep with black
    faces, honeysuckle,
And the wild strawberries scarlet in the hedge
The size for birds' eyes.

We were content to be like castaways,
Idle while the vast sea rushed in
Grinding over the scrupulous sands
Whose every grain swam magnified and clear
Before our downward dazzled gaze,
Gallons of green waves
Spouted over our hot skins their delicious pain
Forcing sharp cries
Out of our heedless mouths,
With endless, endless, soporific roar
Falling on the ear,
On heart, on brain,
Sorrow and thought . . .

We were content to be like castaways,
Recognizing we had found an island
Midway between dangers,
Content, we rested there.

*Joan Barton*

# EMPTY YOUR POCKETS

Empty your pockets, Tom, Dick and Harry,
Strip your identity, leave it behind.
Lawyer, garage-hand, grocer, don't tarry
With your own country, your own kind.

Leave all your letters. Suburb and township,
Green fen and grocery, slipway and bay,
Hot-spring and prairie, smoke stack and coal-tip,
Leave in our keeping while you're away.

Tom, Dick and Harry, plain names and numbers,
Pilot, observer and gunner depart.
Their personal litter only encumbers
Somebody's head, somebody's heart.

*John Pudney*

# News Reel of Embarkation

Where are you going to, laughing men?
For a holiday on the sea?
Laughing, smiling, wonderful men,
Why won't you wait for me?
God, how I love you, men of my race,
As you smile on your way to a war;
How can you do it, wonderful face
Do you not know what's before?
Laugh, laugh, you soldier sons
Joke on your way to the war
For your mothers won't laugh at the sound of
    the guns
And the tales of the filth and the gore.
Smile and joke young sailor Jack
For it's the self-same story:
There'll be no jokes when you come back
And bloody little glory.
(Rhys 1941, 11 and Sinclair, 227)

*Timothy Corsellis*

## *from* ON EMBARKATION

In all the ways of going who can tell
The real from the unjustified farewell?
Women have sobbed when children left for school
Or husbands took the boat train to pursue
Contracts more tenuous than the marriage vow.
But now each railway station makes and breaks
The certain hold and drifts us all apart.
Some women know exactly what's implied.
Ten Years, they say behind their smiling eyes,
Thinking of children, pensions, looks that fade,
The slow forgetfulness that strips the mind
Of its apparel and wears down the thread;
Or maybe when he laughs and bends to make
Her laugh with him she sees that he must die
Because his eyes declare it plain as day.
And it is here, if anywhere, that words
– Debased like money by the same diseases –
Cast off the habitual clichés of fatigue
– The women hoping it will soon blow over,
The fat men saying it depends on Russia –
And all are poets when they say Goodbye
And what they say will live and fructify.

*Alun Lewis*

# I Never Raised My Boy

*I never raised my boy*
*    to be a soldier*
*I brought him up to be*
*    my pride and joy.*
*Who dares to lay a gun*
*    upon his shoulder,*
*And teach him how to kill*
*    another mother's boy.*
*I never raised my boy*
*    to be a soldier.*
*I brought him up to stay*
*    at home with me.*
*There would be no war today,*
*    if every mother would say*
*I never raised my boy*
*    to be a soldier.*

Traditional North Country

## Refugee Blues

Say this city has ten million souls,
Some are living in mansions, some are living in
    holes:
Yet there's no place for us, my dear, yet there's no
    place for us.

Once we had a country and we thought it fair,
Look in the atlas and you'll find it there:
We cannot go there now, my dear, we cannot go
    there now.

In the village churchyard there grows an old yew,
Every spring it blossoms anew:
Old passports can't do that, my dear, old passports
    can't do that.

The consul banged the table and said,
'If you've got no passport you're officially dead';
But we are still alive, my dear, but we are still alive.

Went to a committee; they offered me a chair;
Asked me politely to return next year:
But where shall we go today, my dear, but where
    shall we go today?

Came to a public meeting: the speaker got up and
    said;
'If we let them in, they will steal our daily bread':
He was talking of you and me, my dear, he was
    talking of you and me.

Thought I heard the thunder rumbling in the sky;
It was Hitler over Europe, saying, 'They must die':
O we were in his mind, my dear. O we were in his
    mind.

Saw a poodle in a jacket fastened with a pin.
Saw a door opened and a cat let in:
But they weren't German Jews, my dear, but they
    weren't German Jews.

Went down the harbour and stood upon the quay,
Saw the fish swimming as if they were free:
Only ten feet away, my dear, only ten feet away.

Walked through a wood, saw the birds in the trees;
They had no politicians and sang at their ease:
They weren't the human race, my dear, they
    weren't the human race.

Dreamed I saw a building with a thousand floors,
A thousand windows and a thousand doors:
Not one of them was ours, my dear, not one of
    them was ours.

Stood on a great plain in the falling snow;
Ten thousand soldiers marched to and fro:
Looking for you and me, my dear, looking for you
    and me.

*W. H. Auden*
*March 1939*

# War Poet

I am the man who looked for peace and found
My own eyes barbed.
I am the man who groped for words and found
An arrow in my hand.
I am the builder whose firm walls surround
A slipping land.
When I grow sick or mad
Mock me not nor chain me:
When I reach for the wind
Cast me not down:
Though my face is a burnt book
And a wasted town.

*Sidney Keyes*

# Martial Cadenza

## I

Only this evening I saw again low in the sky
The evening star, at the beginning of winter, the
    star
That in spring will crown every western horizon,
Again . . . as if it came back, as if life came back,
Not in a later son, a different daughter, another
    place,
But as if evening found us young, still young,
Still walking in a present of our own.

## II

It was like sudden time in a world without time,
This world, this place, the street in which I was,
Without time: as that which is not has no time,
Is not, or is of what there was, is full
Of the silence before the armies, armies without
Either trumpets or drums, the commanders mute,
    the arms
On the ground, fixed fast in profound defeat.

# III

What had this star to do with the world it lit,
With the blank skies over England, over France
And above the German camps? It looked apart.
Yet it is this that shall maintain – Itself
Is time, apart from any past, apart
From any future, the ever-living and being,
The ever-breathing and moving, the constant fire,

# IV

The present close, the present realized,
Not the symbol but that for which the symbol
    stands,
The vivid thing in the air that never changes,
Though the air change. Only this evening I saw it
    again,
At the beginning of winter, and I walked and
    talked
Again, and lived and was again, and breathed again
And moved again and flashed again, time flashed
    again.

*Wallace Stevens*

# Mail Call

The letters always just evade the hand.
One skates like a stone into a beam, falls like a bird.
Surely the past from which the letters rise
Is waiting in the future, past the graves?
The soldiers are all haunted by their lives.

Their claims upon their kind are paid in paper
That establishes a presence, like a smell.
In letters and dreams they see the world.
They are waiting: and the years contract
To an empty hand, to one unuttered sound –

The soldier simply wishes for his name.

*Randall Jarrell*

# A Lullaby

For wars his life and half a world away
The soldier sells his family and days.
He learns to fight for freedom and the State;
He sleeps with seven men within six feet.

He picks up matches and he cleans out plates;
Is lied to like a child, cursed like a beast.
They crop his head, his dog tags ring like sheep
As his stiff limbs shift wearily to sleep.

Recalled in dreams or letters, else forgot,
His life is smothered like a grave, with dirt;
And his dull torment mottles like a fly's
The lying amber of the histories.

*Randall Jarrell*

# ALL DAY IT HAS RAINED

All day it has rained, and we on the edge of the
　　moors
Have sprawled in our bell-tents, moody and dull as
　　boors,
Groundsheets and blankets spread on the muddy
　　ground
And from the first grey wakening we have found

No refuge from the skirmishing fine rain
And the wind that made the canvas heave and flap
And the taut wet guy-ropes ravel out and snap.
All day the rain has glided, wave and mist and
　　dream,
Drenching the gorse and heather, a gossamer stream
Too light to stir the acorns that suddenly
Snatched from their cups by the wild south-westerly
Pattered against the tent and our upturned
　　dreaming faces.
And we stretched out, unbuttoning our braces,
Smoking a Woodbine, darning dirty socks,
Reading the Sunday papers – I saw a fox
And mentioned it in the note I scribbled home; –

And we talked of girls and dropping bombs on Rome,
And thought of the quiet dead and the loud celebrities
Exhorting us to slaughter, and the herded refugees;
– Yet thought softly, morosely of them, and as
    indifferently
As of ourselves or those whom we
For years have loved, and will again
Tomorrow maybe love; but now it is the rain
Possesses us entirely, the twilight and the rain.

And I can remember nothing dearer or more to my
    heart
Than the children I watched in the woods on Saturday
Shaking down burning chestnuts for the schoolyard's
    merry play
Or the shaggy patient dog who followed me
By Sheet and Steep and up the wooded scree
To the Shoulder o' Mutton where Edward Thomas
    brooded long
On death and beauty – till a bullet stopped his song.

*Alun Lewis*

— 24 —

# Lessons of the War (To Alan Michell)

*Vixi duellis nuper idoneus*
*Et militavi non sine gloria*

*I – Naming of Parts*

Today we have naming of parts. Yesterday,
We had daily cleaning. And tomorrow morning,
We shall have what to do after firing. But today,
Today we have naming of parts. Japonica
Glistens like coral in all of the neighbouring
    gardens
        And today we have naming of parts.

This is the lower sling swivel. And this
Is the upper sling swivel, whose use you will see
When you are given your slings. And this is the
    piling swivel,
Which in your case you have not got. The
    branches
Hold in the gardens their silent, eloquent gestures,
        Which in our case we have not got.

This is the safety-catch, which is always released
With an easy flick of the thumb. And please do not
    let me
See anyone using his finger. You can do it quite
    easy
If you have any strength in your thumb. The
    blossoms
Are fragile and motionless, never letting anyone see
      Any of them using their finger.

And this you can see is the bolt. The purpose of
    this
Is to open the breech, as you see We can slide it
Rapidly backwards and forwards; we call this
Easing the spring. And rapidly backwards and
    forwards
The early bees are assaulting and fumbling the
    flowers:
      They call it easing the Spring

They call it easing the Spring; it is perfectly easy
If you have any strength in your thumb: like the
   bolt,
And the breech, and the cocking-piece, and the
   point of balance,
Which in our case we have not got; and the
   almond-blossom
Silent in all of the gardens and the bees going
   backwards and forwards,
   For today we have naming of parts.

*Henry Reed*

# First News Reel: September 1939

It was my war, though it ended
When I was ten: could I know or guess
What the talking really said?
– 'Over the top. At the front.
Sealed-with-a-loving-kiss.
Train-loads of wounded men
At the old seaside station.
Two million dead' –
Child of the nightmare-crying 'Never again'.
The same 'I' sits here now
In this silent throng
Watching with dull surprise
Guns limbering to the line
Through umber sheaves,
Guns topped with dappled boys
And crowned with beckoning leaves,
Like floats for some harvest home
Of corn or wine;
A self removed and null
Doubting the eye that sees
The gun in its green bower,
Yet meticulously records

At each load, discharge, recoil,
How the leaves spin from the trees
In an untimely shower
Over the sunlit fields, and are whirled away
To the edge of the sky.
No mud. No wounds. No tears.
No nightmare cries. Is it possible
It could be different this time?
Far-off that passing bell
Tolls 'Different.
Yes always different. Always the same':
As the guns roar and recoil
And the leaves that spin from the trees
Deck boys for a festival.

*Joan Barton*

# BOMBED CHURCH

The heart of the church is broken
Chancel cracked across and
Gone the fragrant-swinging boys.
Echoes are hymnals
Shadows the congregation.
All over London now the spires
May not aspire, and steeples
Are laid as low as the lowest peoples.
Bats descend and flap
If the rusty verger shuffles back.
Once, he told me. Once, he said
In a whisper,
He heard a black owl chant the lesson.

*Elizabeth Berridge*

# Cunard Liner 1940

Now, for the last time, total solitude.
The ship hangs between explosion and quiet
   forward driving,
The faces of the passengers are grave.
Oh what is this sobriety which so denudes us
Of the sarcastic cough, the cackling laughter,
The thin flirtation and the importance of black
   coffee after?
Of course, we are all being British, all being
   ourselves,
All knowing we carry Empire on our shoulders:
But even so, we are exceptionally grave.
Voices: 'My husband's heavily insured.'
'I said to stewardess, get baby into the boat!'
'I carry pneumonia tablets in my old army bag.'

Yes, friends, but if we had no time to scramble
For babies, tablets and insurance papers,
What would the U-boat's dart, the spurting mine
Mean to each one of us? The end of *what*?

The end of helpless dignity for the army officer!
The end of dancing for the golden girl:
The end of suckling babies for the mother:
The end of study for the gangling youth:
The end of profit for the business men:
The end of brave sea-faring for the crew:
But for so many it would be the end of nothing,
Of nothing nicely done and dearly cherished.

And for myself? oh darling, for myself
It would be life's most true and fatal end;
It would be the conclusion in my brain
And my most spirited heart and my fair body
Of you – the last rich consciousness of you.

*Phyllis Shand Allfrey*

# 7 October, 1940

One does not have to worry if we die:
Whoever dies, One does not have to bother
Because inside Her there is still another
And, that one wasted too, She yet replies
'Nothing can tire out Nature – here's another!'
  Fecundity par excellence is here,
  Lying in labour even on the bier.

Maternity's the holiest thing on earth
(No man who's prudent as well as wise
Concerns himself with what is in the skies);
Drain-deep below the slums another birth
  Sets angels singing – the other noise you hear
  May be the Warning, may be the All Clear.

Comfort ye My people! These reflections
Should help them die politely who must die,
And reconcile those left behind, who sigh
For loss of children or some near connections –
  Reflect! There is no need for grief nor gloom,
  Nature has ever another in Her womb.

Teeming and steaming hordes who helter–skelter
Stampede the city streets, to herd together
Angry and scared, in dark, in wintry weather –
Above ground still? Fear not, there's one deep
   shelter
      Open alike in Free and Fascist State,
      Vast, private, silent and inviolate.

*Valentine Ackland*

# DUNKIRK

For many days it seemed as if the sky
Held back its breath in anguish, and the sea
Seemed frozen by our fear, for storms meant death
To countless thousands who this calm set free.

Our whole world dwindled to that narrow beach;
We watched a miracle with hearts of stone,
Then, awestruck with relief, we turned once more
To seek for friends – and found ourselves alone.

*Mary Désirée Anderson*
*M.D.A., Lady Cox, lived in London during the war.*

# PILOT STATION, HARWICH

Landmarks of sorts there always were,
Flamborough Head, Immingham, Southwold –
Sea-marks as well, the buoys
Marking the channel where E-boats,
Engines idling, waited for us, all contacts
Muffled. But they were mere signposts,
Not aspects of arrival –

No, the real landmark that made
The pulse quicken, coming up on deck
On a summer morning, was the black
And white pagoda of the Trinity House
Pilot Station, exotic to us as Konorak
Or Madurai. Anchoring there,
We could look down from above
At the launches swishing up the estuary
With signals and mail, Wrens at the helm
In bell-bottoms, their lovely hair flying.
It was the nearest we ever got to love.

*Alan Ross*

# THE TRAINS

Tunnelling through the night, the trains pass
in a splendour of power, with a sound like thunder
shaking the orchards, waking
the young from a dream, scattering like glass
the old men's sleep; laying
a black trail over the still bloom of the orchards.
The trains go north with guns.

Strange primitive piece of flesh, the heart laid quiet
hearing their cry pierce through its thin-walled
   cave
recalls the forgotten tiger
and leaps awake in its old panic riot;
and how shall mind be sober,
since blood's red thread still binds us fast in history?
Tiger, you walk through all our past and future,
troubling the children's sleep; laying
a reeking trail across our dream of orchards.

Racing on iron errands, the trains go by,
and over the white acres of our orchards
hurl their wild summoning cry, their animal cry . . .
the trains go north with guns.

*Judith Wright*

# BOMBING AT NOON OF SCHOOL AT LEWISHAM

Flowers were blooming at noonday
In a city garden on earth.
Children fair, happy and gay,
Laughing aloud in their mirth.
Out of the skies above them,
With never a warning wail,
Swept a storm of thunder and lightning,
With murderous steel for hail.
It mowed them down like a reaper,
And thunderbolts crashed and crushed,
Bruising, and killing, and maiming,
Wherever the storm-clouds brushed.

Christ walked in the garden at eventide,
And in wrath beheld the wreck.
He said 'It were better for him who did this deed,
That he were drowned in the deepest sea,
A millstone about his neck.
For he hath offended my little ones,
In their innocent happy play.
But leave to Me the Vengeance,
It is mine, I will repay.'

We buried the broken blossoms,
In a grave in the warm brown earth,
But Christ gathered up the plantlets,
And took them to Paradise.
He planted them all in a garden fair,
Where flows the River of Life.
They are growing there and will bloom again,
In the loving Father's care.
Where no storms come near, or death or fear,
They will wait for those they left,
And will welcome them in at the garden gate,
United for evermore.

*May Hill*
*January 1943*

# From a Letter to America on a Visit to Sussex: Spring 1942

How simply violent things
Happen, is strange.
How strange it was to see
In the soft Cambridge sky our Squadron's wings,
And hear the huge hum in the familiar grey.
And it was odd today
On Ashdown Forest that will never change,
To find a gunner in the gorse, flung down,
Well-camouflaged (and bored and lion-brown).
A little further by those twisted trees
(As if it rose on humped preposterous seas
Out of a Book of Hours) up a bank
Like a large dragon, purposeful though drunk,
Heavily lolloped, swayed and sunk,
A tank.
All this because manoeuvres had begun.
But now, but soon,
At home on any usual afternoon,
High overhead
May come the Erinyes winging.
Or here the boy may lie beside his gun,

His mud-brown tunic gently staining red,
While larks get on with their old job of singing.

*Frances Cornford*

# THE SUNLIGHT ON THE GARDEN

The sunlight on the garden
Hardens and grows cold,
We cannot cage the minute
Within its nets of gold,
When all is told
We cannot beg for pardon.

Our freedom as free lances
Advances towards its end;
The earth compels, upon it
Sonnets and birds descend;
And soon, my friend,
We shall have no time for dances.

The sky was good for flying
Defying the church bells
And every evil iron
Siren and what it tells:
The earth compels,
We are dying, Egypt, dying

And not expecting pardon,
Hardened in heart anew,
But glad to have sat under
Thunder and rain with you,
And grateful too
For sunlight on the garden.

*Louis MacNeice*

# SONNET, 1940

The point where beauty and intelligence meet,
Where intersecting lines cross and divide –
Happy were I to lie between those feet
Or by that rare and warm and lovely side –
You are the centre of my moving world,
The cold ideal to which I daily move
Although iron flags of battle are unfurled –
You are not yet, though might still be, my love.
And I, before the happy tough battalions
Engulf me or the frozen seas of Norway,
Have still my dreams of cities and of dalliance,
But most of you as standing in a doorway,
Who might, though I so dissipate my life,
Be mistress or, fear of the young, a wife.

*Gavin Ewart*

## LEAVE POEM

O let the days spin out
In leisure, as the clouds pass;
Weave webs of shadow
Across the grass.

Let nothing touch me now,
But the minty mountain air,
Sun, wind and your fingers
Through my hair.

And when the hills grow cold
Outside, lock out the night,
Tell me long tales and stir
The fire bright.

For I would be bastioned here
Against the constant hum
Of streets and men and ships
Whence we have come.

So let the days spin out
In magic hours and laughter
That I may hold the thought
Long, long after.

*Anne Bulley*

# LEAVE

If for a single hour I might be free
    And that one hour might all be spent with you,
    What should we say, my love? what should we do
In such a little hour as that would be?
Words, after so long, would not come to me;
    Kisses would be but torture, being so few
    And yet recalling all the joy we knew
Before I went to war beyond the sea.
But if I took you to the edge of land
    Where we might watch the sea spread wide away
    And the slant waves along the pebbles creep,
Then by the white brink of the tide we'd stand
    And press each other's hand, and nothing say,
    But know the silence coming from the deep.

*John Buxton*

# THE BLACK-OUT

I never feared the darkness as a child,
For then night's plumy wings that wrapped me
  round
Seemed gentle, and all earthly sound,
Whether man's movement or the wild,
Small stirrings of the beasts and trees, was kind,
So I was well contented to be blind.

But now the darkness is a time of dread,
Of stumbling, fearful progress, when one thinks,
With angry fear, that those dull amber chinks,
Which tell of life where all things else seem dead,
Are full of menace as a tiger's eyes
That watch our passing, hungry for the prize.

Over all Europe lies this shuddering night.
Sometimes it quivers like a beast of prey,
All tense to spring, or, trembling, turns at bay
Knowing itself too weak for force or flight,
And in all towns men strain their eyes and ears,
Like hunted beasts, for warning of their fears.

*Mary Désirée Anderson*

# I'VE FINISHED MY BLACK-OUT
(The Song of a Triumphant Housewife)

I've finished my Black-out!
    There's paint on the carpet and glue on my hair
    There's a saw in the bathroom and spills on the
      stair,
    And a drawing pin lost in the seat of a chair,
      But I've finished my Black-out.

The bedrooms are draped with funereal black
Except for the little one facing the back,
And that we have had to nail up with a sack,
      But I've finished my Black-out!

      Oh, I've finished my Black-out!
Policemen and wardens may peer and may pry,
And enemy planes may look down from the sky,
But they won't see a pin-prick however they try,
      For I've finished my Black-out!

*Anon.*

## BLACK-OUT

Night comes now
Without the artistry of hesitation, the surprising
Last minute turn-aside into a modulation,
Without the rising
Final assertion of promise before the fall.

Darkness now
Comes by routine of cardboard shutter, rattle of
    curtain,
Comes like a sentence everyone's learnt to utter,
Undoubted and certain,
Too stupid to interest anyone at all.

*Valentine Ackland*

# BLITZ

In London now Death holds high festival.
The clustered candelabra of the flares,
High in the darkly thrumming vault of heaven,
Hang motionless, then slowly, slowly, drop
Towards the shrinking darkness of men's homes.

In parody of dawn the eastern sky
Flames with the ghastly beauty of great fires.
The moonbeam tentacles of searchlights grope
Through baffling cirrus, while the moon herself
Seems to grow smaller, shrinking from the earth,
Her brightness reddened by the reek of war.

Strangely unreal seems the roar of guns,
The long-continued crash of falling walls,
With snake-like sibilance of splintered glass,
And slowly swelling mushrooms of black smoke
Rising from bursting bombs. With all of these
We are familiar through a thousand films,
And scarce believe them to be bitter truth.
Strangely unreal too the ageless faces
Of those who struggle out of shattered homes;

Faces expressionless through fear and dust,
Dust that was once the fabric of their homes.

I've seen old women, trembling from the shock,
Yet angry only that their limbs should thus
Betray the fear their smiling lips denied.
I've seen young children watch the solid walls
Bend inwards with the blast and then recoil;
Seen their eyes wide with terror and their mouths
Closed far too tightly for such tender lips,
Yet never sound came from them in their fear.

I have seen Death hold festival tonight,
With hideous beauty of dark ritual,
And yet, as plainly, read a Covenant
That Man's unconquerable kindliness
Shall master hate as surely as the dawn
Makes dim the terrors of Death's Beltane fires.

*Mary Désirée Anderson*

## Autumn Blitz

Unshaken world! Another day of light
After the human chaos of the night;
Although a heart in mendless horror grieves,
What calmly yellow, gently falling leaves!

*Frances Cornford*

# OCTOBER 1940

When leaves like guineas start to fall
And sycamore and elm begin
Red tears to shed, then Autumn's in
And Summer gone beyond recall.

Thick, thick they fell from London trees
In years that seem an age ago;
They cantered then down Rotten Row
And ran down Broad Walk with the breeze.

The children laughed to see them run
And caught them in their merry flight
And we were glad, for their delight
Beneath the thin October sun.

But there's another fall today,
When bombs instead of leaves come down
To drive our children out of town
And us to ground. We will repay.

*Anon.*

# AEROPLANES

A dragonfly
in a flecked grey sky.

Its silvered planes
break the wide and still
harmony of space.

Around it shells
flash
their fumes
burgeoning to blooms
smoke-lilies that float
along the sky.

Among them darts
a dragonfly.

*Herbert Read*

# FOR JOHNNY

Do not despair
For Johnny-Head-in-Air;
He sleeps as sound
As Johnny-underground.

Fetch out no shroud
For Johnny-in-the-Cloud,
And keep your tears
For him in after years.

Better by far
For Johnny-the-bright-star
To keep your head
And see his children fed.

*John Pudney*

## IMMENSITY

You go at night into immensity,
Leaving this green earth, where hawthorn flings
Pale stars on hedgerows, and our serenity
Is twisted into strange shapes; my heart never sings
Now on spring mornings, for you fly at nightfall
From this earth I know
Toward the clear stars, and over all
Those dark seas and waiting towns you go;
And when you come to me
There are fearful dreams in your eyes,
And remoteness. Oh, God! I see
How far away you are,
Who may so soon meet death beneath an alien star.

*Mabel Esther Allan*
*Late 1940*

# HIGH FLIGHT

Oh! I have slipped the surly bonds of Earth
And danced the skies on laughter-silvered wings;
Sunward I've climbed, and joined the tumbling
    mirth
Of sun-split clouds – and done a hundred things
You have not dreamed of – wheeled and soared
    and swung
High in the sunlit silence. Hov'ring there,
I've chased the shouting wind along, and flung
My eager craft through footless halls of air . . .

Up, up the long delirious burning blue
I've topped the wind-swept heights with easy grace
Where never lark, or even eagle flew –
And while with silent lifting mind I've trod
The high untrespassed sanctity of space,
Put out my hand and touched the face of God.

*John Magee*

# THE HEART TO CARRY ON

Every morning from this home
I go to the aerodrome
And at evening I return
Save when work is to be done.
Then we share the separate night
Half a continent apart.

Many endure worse than we:
Division means by years and seas.
Home and lover are contained,
Even cursed within their breast.

Leaving you now, with this kiss
May your sleep tonight be blest,
Shielded from the heart's alarms
Until morning I return.
Pray tomorrow I may be
Close, my love, within these arms,
And not lie dead in Germany.

*Bertram Warr*

# UNSEEN FIRE

This is a damned inhuman sort of war.
I have been fighting in a dressing-gown
Most of the night; I cannot see the guns,
The sweating gun-detachments or the planes;
I sweat down here before a symbol thrown
Upon a screen, sift facts, initiate
Swift calculations and swift orders; wait
For the precise split-second to order fire.

We chant our ritual words; beyond the phones
A ghost repeats the orders to the guns:
One Fire . . . Two Fire . . . ghosts answer: the guns
    roar
Abruptly; and an aircraft waging war
Inhumanly from nearly five miles height
Meets our bouquet of death – and turns sharp
    right.

*R. N. Currey*

# The Click of the Garden Gate

I hear the click of the garden gate
But it is not he
He comes no more either early or late
To his dinner or tea
He is far away in an Air Force Camp
Learning to fight
(I wonder if his blankets are damp
And if he sleeps well at night)

Not twenty years when went away
Just a boy
He may never again come back to stay
To delight and annoy
Will what he has gained balance what he has lost?
He will change
Will his growth to manhood improve him most?
Or make him change?

I open the casement into his room
So tidy and neat
And the sun shines in and chases the gloom
And the wind blows sweet
Ready for him when, early or late
He comes back home to the sea
I hear the click of the garden gate
But it is not he.
(Perhaps it is Rene coming to tea!)

*May Hill*
*December 1940*

# 'The Casualties Were Small'

When Winton Aerodrome was bombed
The 'Casualties were small'
Just your son, and my son, and little widow
    Brown's son,
The youngest of them all.

And your son was your eldest lad,
Handsome and straight and tall.
A model for your younger sons,
Beloved by you all.

And Mrs Brown's, her youngest boy
Her sole support, and stay.
So like his father, all her joy
Was quenched, on that dark day.

And mine, my only son and pride
So loved and dear to all.
The blast of bombs spread far and wide
Tho' 'the casualties were small'.

*May Hill*
*September 1941*

# AIRCREW

The grasshopper Wellington comes to land.
The hand on the levers is not my hand.
Mine are more struck to earth and sand.

Permission to land on the rising ground.
Bandaged the casual aerial wound.
The pub on the hill has change for a pound.

Lying at last on the hugging bed.
The vertical toes and the parallel head.
There was something the girl in the photo said.

Born for war of born for a game.
The factories are burning, but no one's to blame.
In a thousand years they'll be burning the same.

In the morning they land in the black ages field.
Sun in our air, touch down, and are concealed.
On an old earth: their sickness will be healed.

*Brian Allwood*

# PILOT

The airman has nothing to say about this.
The moon is rising and she is not his,
Or wings are caking with malignant ice.

Distant the point where different language speaks.
The hours are minutes and the years are weeks.
The slow gulls wander; and the tracer streaks.

Has nothing to say, and this is done.
At night the long youth of the flaring gun;
Against the great raiders, the great sun.

Returning now the dawn lets him be safe:
No one has really asked him for life,
Eating eggs and bacon with a fork and knife.

*Brian Allwood*

# A Gunner's Day

A gunner's day is never done,
Up at dawn before the sun.
With the roar of engines in his head,
Wishing he could have stayed in bed.

Chow at four, fried eggs and such,
Won't have time to eat too much.
Briefing at five, the crew is all there,
And ever anxious to be up in the air.

See to your chute, ammunition and guns,
For the boys all know its not for fun.
Jerry will be there high up in the blue,
Waiting for someone, perhaps for you.

Take off at six or maybe at six–thirty,
Hope no one has a gun that is dirty.
Form with the group at 12,000 feet,
See the formation, they really look neat.

Put on your mask the air is getting thin,
Off to battle, some with a grin.
Were over the water, now test your guns,
Enemy coast, here comes the fun.

Flak at six and flak at twelve,
Look out! you hear the bombardier yell.
Here come Fighters, coming in low
Maybe they're ours, don't shoot till you know.

P-58's and P-38's
Our escort is here, they're never late.
They're fighting fools, each man and his ship.
There is never a Jerry they couldn't whip.

The air is cold just fifty below,
Turn up the heat so you don't freeze a toe.
A sharp lookout boys, the target is near
We don't care to meet the enemy here.

There is the target, plenty of flak,
Bombs Away! Boys now we turn back.
Coming out of the sun, there are enemy ships,
Aim true boys, we've still got more trips.

There goes one down, another one too.
Our Fighters are busy to see none get through.
There one flames in the sky, as another goes down
The pilot bails out, he makes it safe to the ground.

Then in our tail our guns start to roar,
There's blood on your guns, you shoot as before.
Your ship is hit but still flies through the air,
You think of your loved ones and whisper a
    prayer.

Smoke from the target leaps high in the sky,
We'll show the damn Jerries we know how to fly,
The Fighters have left us, the few that are left
Our Fighters got some, we got the rest.

We've been up six hour, two hours to go
Though were doing 200, it seems very slow.
England at last, the tail gunners learn
We think of our buddies who will not return.

We're over the field the crew gives a sigh
We have finished another to do or to die.
Wheels touched the ground with a screech and a
    bump,
Our ship brought us back over the hump.

We're tired, dirty, thirsty and sore,
The sun has gone down an hour before.
First clean your guns, do it good boys
For that gun's life is mine or yours.

A sandwich and coffee, your chute you turn in,
Down to the briefing room, turn in your gun.
Two meals, both in the darkness of night,
Get on your nerves, but you're still ready to fight.

The mess hall is warm in the cold of night,
You sit down to eat, talk between bites.
You talk of Fighters, theirs and ours, too
And of the boys that didn't get through.

Of ships going down exploding in air,
The bullets that missed your head by a hair.
Your ship full of holes, guess Joe is in bed,
He has a flak fragment lodged in his head.

Then head for your sack at nine or ten.
A letter from home, another from her.
I love you she wrote, then you know you've won,
A gunner's day is never done.

*Anon.*

# Raiders' Dawn

Softly the civilized
Centuries fall,
Paper on paper,
Peter on Paul.

And lovers waking
From the night –
Eternity's masters,
Slaves of Time –
Recognize only
The drifting white
Fall of small faces
In pits of lime.

Blue necklace left
On a charred chair
Tells that Beauty
Was startled there.

*Alun Lewis*

# AFTER NIGHT OFFENSIVE

Glowed through the violet petal of the sky
Like a death's-head the calm summer moon
And all the distance echoed with owl-cry.

Hissing the white waves of grass unsealed
Peer of moon on metal, hidden men,
As the wind foamed deeply through the field.

Rooted to soil, remote and faint as stars,
Looking to neither side, they lay all night
Sunken in the murmurous seas of grass.

No flare burned upwards: never sound was shed
But lulling cries of owls beyond the world.
As wind and moon played softly with the dead.

*James Farrar*

# Parachute Descent

Snap back the canopy,
Pull out the oxygen tube,
Flick the harness pin
And slap out into the air
Clear of the machine.

Did you ever dream when you were young
Of floating through the air, hung
Between the clouds and the gay
Be-blossomed land?
Did you ever stand and say,
'To sit and think and be alone
In the middle of the sky
Is my one most perfect wish'?

That was a fore-knowing;
You knew that some day
To satiate an inward crave
You must play with the wave
Of a cloud. And shout aloud
In the clean air,
The untouched-by-worldly-things-and-mean air,
With exhilarated living.

You knew that you must float
From the sun above the clouds
To the gloom beneath, from a world
Of rarefied splendour to one
Of cheapened dirt, close-knit
In its effort to encompass man
In death.

So you can stay in the clouds, boy,
You can let your soul go onwards,
You have no ties on earth,
You could never have accomplished
Anything. Your ideas and ideals
Were too high. So you can stay
In the sky, boy, and have no fear.

*David Bourne*

# AIRMAN'S WIFE

Carols a later thrush remindingly
But neither I nor twilight can turn you away.
So I watch you, and you watch aircraft on the rim
Of a green pool of sky, heavily one by one
Leave the just-twinkling flare-path, fierce with
    power
To surge black-bellied above us here
And sing away to darkness.

Though they have less humanity than stars,
The red remote lights circling while we pause,
That must not frighten you.
The faint cry of engines lost in night
Shall have no echo here. We young do not forget
Sunlight that ripples over the bright hours of day
Blessing our indivisibility . . .

But always, watching you, I understand
How much of life is evening, engine-sound
And being crucified alone at night.

*James Farrar*
*Spring 1943*

## MECHANIZATION

Only seven months have passed but what a change
    they've made.
Remember how it used to be when troops got on
    parade?
'See those bits are fitted right!
See those girths are tight!
Mind you shake the blankets out before you put
    'em on!'
How the nose-bands caught the light, how the
    steel-work shone!

All that's very different now. We dress like garage
   hands;
Gone now the clink of bit and spur; no trumpets
   now, no bands.
'Petrol, oil and water right?
All the wheel-nuts tight?
Did you check the levels up before you got
   aboard?'
No more, alas, the head-tossed foam, the fretful
   foot that pawed:
Oh glory that was Tetrarch's might, oh drabness
   that is Ford!

*E. F. Gosling*

# 'Non-walking wounded will be left with civilians where possible.'

*Wellington was reputed to have said,*
*'Gentlemen, the difference between a retreat and a rout,*
*is that in a rout the wounded are left behind.'*

Madame had told us she'd take them,
So on mattress, bed-spring, door,
We carried them clumsy, tender,
And laid them, on the Pension's cellar floor;
We lit the four tall candles
We'd nicked from the shell-shocked church;
We left them some water and toffees
    and some really horrible fags;
Each one of us felt he was half a man
As we guessed from their eyes that they knew it
    was lies
The yarn that I told, and the day grew old
    and the evening's shelling began.

Madame came down with her walking cane
Testing each cellar stair;
She had a cameo brooch, and a fine proud comb
In the back of her silvering hair;
She creaked me an old world curtsy
When I gave her my smartest salute;
She bent by the ginger-haired corporal –
The one with the hideous burn –
Looked up and said in her Flemish slang
I'd learned at my Grandma's knee,
'You bloody lot get moving, one day you will
 return!'
So we hurried out to the stink of rout
 and the sight of the blessèd sea!

*Douglas Street*
*Belgium, May 1940*

## 25-POUNDER

O little dragon
Best seen from behind,
You have no paragon
In dragon-kind
For you can kill
Wherever you will
Without the bother
Of climbing a hill.

This much you have
In common with love.

*Francis Scarfe*

# Firing with Heavy Guns

They laugh like fallen archangels, these four guns,
Utter their searing blasphemies of flame
And thunder that seeks to take in vain the name
And power of God; they flash hot vivid suns

From every side, and all four firing at once
In one clean salvo separately clout
Your head from side to side; they laugh and shout
And make the sandbags leap with their loud tones.

They are the fallen archangels, this the hour
In which they taste some memory of the power
With which they stormed the frontiers of heaven.
The four rounds burst together, seven miles high,
Quite close – good shooting, but they have not
    even
Begun to climb the immense heights of the sky.

*R. N. Currey*

# THE TARN

'We'd better split now. Keep behind the trees
Down to the tarn's edge. If there's a plane, come
    back
And meet me here: don't fire, they'll have MGs.
– We'll need to get as close as we can get.'
I heard the silky rustle of the skis
And stood stock-still, listening till it had gone.
I threaded one stick through the ring and strap
Of the other, and held them so in my left hand.
I cocked my tommy-gun – so loud, so loud
That little click! Zigzag from tree to tree,
Straining for any other sound beyond
The swishing of my skis, I ran to the tarn.
Between the black, still branches of a spruce
I looked across the ice: only the wind
Had made black random furrows in the snow.

*John Buxton*
*Norway 1940*

# HOW TO KILL

Under the parabola of a ball,
a child turning into a man,
I looked into the air too long.
The ball fell in my hand, it sang
in the closed fist: *Open Open*
*Behold a gift designed to kill.*

Now in my dial of glass appears
the soldier who is going to die.
He smiles, and moves about in ways
his mother knows, habits of his.
The wires touch his face: I cry
NOW. Death, like a familiar, hears

and look, has made a man of dust
of a man of flesh. This sorcery
I do. Being damned, I am amused
to see the centre of love diffused
and the waves of love travel into vacancy.
How easy it is to make a ghost.

The weightless mosquito touches
her tiny shadow on the stone,
and with how like, how infinite
a lightness, man and shadow meet.
They fuse. A shadow is a man
when the mosquito death approaches.

*Keith Douglas*

# CASSINO REVISITED

This place did catch a vast pox from off the Moon;
Craters and wrinkle all are here,
And we are travellers from another Time;
This place still keeps its own infected counsel;
The most thin atmospheres of loneliness and fear
Still make a heavy labour for the heart;
Yet tribes, I know, lived here, those loved and
    clumsy tribes
That men call regiments; one tribe would start
The day with telling of its beads; the men of one
Would talk of killings with the knives, and rum;
Yet others talked of the clean and unchronicled
    Antipodes,
Of pasture and a blue haze of trees;
Some had left their private silken skies behind,
Folded neatly with the storemen, out of mind;
And all read letters smelling of the mules,
And talked of two myth-planets, Rome and
    Home;
For battle cries they used shy word – 'Perhaps' or
    'Fairly soon'.

*Douglas Street*

# LANDSCAPE WITH FIGURES

1
Perched on a great fall of air
a pilot or angel looking down
on some eccentric chart, the plain
dotted with the useless furniture
discerns crouching on the sand vehicles
squashed dead or still entire, stunned
like beetles: scattered wingcases and
legs, heads, show when the haze settles.
But you who like Thomas come
to poke fingers in the wounds
find monuments, and metal posies:
on each disordered tomb
the steel is torn into fronds
by the lunatic explosive.

**2**

On scrub and sand the dead men wriggle
in their dowdy clothes. They are mimes
who express silence and futile aims
enacting this prone and motionless struggle
at a queer angle to the scenery
crawling on the boards of the stage like walls
deaf to the one who opens his mouth and calls
silently. The décor is terrible tracery
of iron. The eye and mouth of each figure
bear the cosmetic blood and hectic
colours death has the only list of.
A yard more, and my little finger
could trace the maquillage of these stony actors
I am the figure writhing on the backcloth.

*Keith Douglas*

# LETTER FROM ITALY

From large red bugs, a refugee,
I make my bed beneath the sky,
safe from the crawling enemy
though not secure from nimbler flea.
Late summer darkness comes, and now
I see again the homely Plough
and wonder: do you also see
the seven stars as well as I?
And it is good to find a tie
of seven stars from you to me.
Lying on deck, on friendly seas,
I used to watch, with no delight,
new unsuggestive stars that light
the tedious Antipodes.
Now in a hostile land I lie,
but share with you these ancient high
familiar named divinities.
Perimeters have bounded me,
sad rims of desert and of sea,
the famous one around Tobruk,
and now barbed wire, which way I look,
except above – the Pleiades.

*Robert Garioch*

# EMBARKATION, 1942

In undetected trains we left our land
At evening secretly, from wayside stations.
None knew our place of parting; no pale hand
Waved as we went, not one friend said farewell.
But grouped on weed-grown platforms
Only a few officials holding watches
Noted the stealthy hour of our departing,
And, as we went, turned back to their hotel.

With blinds drawn down we left the things we
    know,
The simple fields, the homely ricks and yards;
Passed willows greyly bunching to the moon
And English towns. But in our blindfold train
Already those were far and long ago,
Stored quiet pictures which the mind must keep:
We saw them not. Instead we played at cards,
Or strangely dropped asleep.

Then in a callow dawn we stood in lines
Like foreigners on bare and unknown quays,
Till someone bravely into the hollow of waiting
Cast a timid wisp of song;
It moved along the lines of patient soldiers
Like a secret passed from mouth to mouth
And slowly gave us ease;
In our whispered singing courage was set free,
We were banded once more and strong.
So we sang as our ship set sail,
Sang our own songs, and leaning on the rail
Waved to the workmen on the slipping quay
And then again to us for fellowship.

*John Jarmain*

## *from* ELEGY FOR AN UNKNOWN SOLDIER

There was a time when I would magnify
His ending: scatter words as if I wept
Tears not of my own but man's; there was a time.
But not now so. He died of a common sickness.

Awkward at school, he could not master sums.
Could you expect him then to understand
The miracle and menace of his body
That grew as mushrooms grow from dusk to dawn?

He had the weight, though, for a football scrum,
And thought it fine to listen to the cheering
And drink beer with the boys, telling them tall
Stories of girls he had never known.

But when the War came he was glad and sorry,
But soon enlisted. Then his mother cried
A little, and his father boasted how
He'd let him go, though needed for the farm.

Likely in Egypt he would find out something
About himself, if flies and drunkenness
And deadly heat could tell him much – until
In his first battle a shell splinter caught him.

So crown him with memorial bronze among
The older dead, child of a mountainous island.
Wings of a tarnished victory shadow him
Who born of silence has burned back to silence.

*James K. Baxter*

# EL ALAMEIN

There are flowers now, they say, at Alamein;
Yes, flowers in the minefields now.
So those that come to view that vacant scene,
Where death remains and agony has been
Will find the lilies grow –
Flowers, and nothing that we know.

So they rang the bells for us and Alamein,
Bells which we could not hear.
And to those that heard the bells what could it
    mean,
The name of loss and pride, El Alamein?
– Not the murk and harm of war.
But their hope, their own warm prayer.

It will become a staid historic name,
That crazy sea of sand!
Like Troy or Agincourt its single fame
Will be the garland for our brow, our claim,
On us a fleck of glory to the end;
And there our dead will keep their holy ground.

But this is not the place that we recall,
The crowded desert crossed with foaming tracks,
The one blotched building, lacking half a wall,
The grey-faced men, sand-powdered over all;
The tanks, the guns, the trucks,
The black, dark-smoking wrecks.

So be it; none but us has known that land;
El Alamein will still be only ours
And those ten days of chaos in the sand.
Others will come who cannot understand,
Will halt beside the rusty minefield wires
and find there, flowers.

*John Jarmain*

# WAR GRAVES AT EL ALAMEIN

When they were little children they explored
Forests dense with dangers, were pursued
By beast, or giant wielding knife or sword
And terrified they found their feet were glued
Firmly to the ground; they could not scream
Or run, yet they were never stabbed or gored
But always woke to find it just a dream.

Years and nightmares later they became
Old enough to put on uniform,
And in parched throats they gagged upon the same
Taste of childhood terror in a storm
Of killing thunder they must battle through.
Now, unimportant pieces in the game,
They sleep and know that last bad dream was true.

*Vernon Scannell*

# ENFIDAVILLE

In the church fallen like dancers
lie the Virgin and St Therese
on little pillows of dust.
The detonations of the last few days
tore down the ornamental plasters
shivered the hands of Christ.

The men and women who moved like candles
in and out of the houses and the streets
are all gone. The white houses are bare
black cages. No one is left to greet
the ghosts tugging at doorhandles
opening doors that are not there.

Now the daylight coming in from the fields
like a labourer, tired and sad,
is peering about among the wreckage, goes
past some corners as though with averted head
not looking at the pain this town holds,
seeing no one move behind the windows.

But already they are coming back; to search
like ants, poking in the debris, finding in it
a bed or a piano and carrying it out.
Who would not love them at this minute?
I seem again to meet
the blue eyes of the images in the church.

*Keith Douglas*
*Tunisia, May 1943*

## *from* BURMA CASUALTY
(To Captain G. T. Morris, Indian Army)

'Your leg must go. Okay?' the surgeon said
'Take it' he said. 'I hate the bloody thing.'
Yet he was terrified – not of the knives
Nor losing that green leg (he'd often wished
He'd had a gun to shoot the damned thing off)
But of the darkness that he knew would come
And bid him enter its deep gates alone.


The nurse would help him and the orderlies.
But did they know? And could a rubber tube
Suck all that darkness out of lungs and heart?
'Open and close your fist – slowly,' the doctor said.
He did so, lying still upon his back.
The whitewashed walls, the windows bright with
  sky
Gathered a brilliant light above his head.
Here was the light, the promise hard and pure,
His wife's sweet body and her wilful eyes.
Her timeless love stooped down to raise him up.
He felt the white walls part – the needle pricked,
'Ten seconds and you'll fade,' the doctor said.

He lay and looked into the snowwhite skies
For all ten seconds means at such a time.
Then through the warped interstices of life
The darkness swept like water through a boat
In gouts and waves of softness, claiming him . . .

He went alone: knew nothing: and returned
Retching and blind with pain, and yet Alive.

*Alun Lewis*

# TROOPSHIP

Now the fish fly, the multiple skies display
Still more astounding patterns, the colours are
More brilliant than fluid paint, the grey more grey.

At dawn I saw a solitary star
Making a wake across the broken sea,
Against the heavens swayed a sable spar.

The hissing of the deep is silence, the
Only noise is our memories.

                    O far
From our desires, at every torrid port,
Between the gem-hung velvet of the waves,
Our sires and grandsires in their green flesh start,
Bend skinny elbows, warn: 'We have no graves.
We passed this way, with good defended ill.
Our virtue perished, evil is prince there still.'

*Roy Fuller*

# A Troopship in the Tropics

Five thousand souls are here and all are bounded
Too easily perhaps by the ostensible purpose,
Steady as the ploughshare cleaving England,
Of this great ship, obedient to its compass.

The sundeck for the children and the officers
Under the awning, watching the midsea blue
Until the nurses pass with a soft excitement
Rustling the talk of passengers and crew.

Deep in the foetid holds the tiered bunks
Hold restless men who sweat and toss and sob;
The gamblers on the hatches, in the corner
The accordionist and barber do their job.

The smell of oranges and excrement
Moves among those who write uneasy letters
Or slouch about and curse the stray dejection
That chafes them with its hard nostalgic fetters.

But everywhere in this sweltering Utopia,
In the bareheaded crowd's two minutes' silence,
In corners where the shadows lie like water,
Are tranquil pools of crystal-clear reflexion.

Time is no mystery now; this torrid blueness
Blazed in a fortnight from the English winter.
Distance is subject to our moods and wishes.
*Only the void of feeling must be filled.*

And as the ship makes peace within herself
The simple donors of goodness with rugged features
Move in the crowd and share their crusts of
     wisdom;
Like does not name her rough undoctored teachers.

Welsh songs surge softly in the circling darkness;
Thoughts sail back like swans to the English winter;
Strange desires drift into the mind;
Time hardens. But the ruthless Now grows kind.

*Alun Lewis*

# Walking Wounded

A mammoth morning moved grey flanks and
    groaned.
In the rusty hedges pale rags of mist hung;
The gruel of mud and leaves in the mauled lane
Smelled sweet, like blood. Birds had died or flown,
Their green and silent attics sprouting now
With branches of leafed steel, hiding round eyes
And ripe grenades ready to drop and burst.
In the ditch at the crossroads the fallen rider lay
Hugging his dead machine and did not stir
At crunch of mortar, tantrum of a Bren
Answering a Spandau's manic jabber.
Then into sight the ambulances came,
Stumbling and churning past the broken farm,
The amputated signpost and smashed trees,
Slow wagonloads of bandaged cries, square trucks
That rolled on ominous wheels, vehicles
Made mythopoeic by their mortal freight
And crimson crosses on the dirty white.
This grave procession passed, though, for a while,
The grinding of their engines could be heard,
A dark noise on the pallor of the morning,

Dark as dried blood; and then it faded, died.
The road was empty, but it seemed to wait –
Like a stage which knows the cast is in the wings –
Wait for a different traffic to appear.
The mist still hung in snags from dripping thorns;
Absent-minded guns still sighed and thumped.
And then they came, the walking wounded,
Straggling the road like convicts loosely chained,
Dragging at ankles exhaustion and despair.
Their heads were weighted down by last night's
    lead,
And eyes still drank the dark. They trailed the
    night
Along the morning road. Some limped on sticks;
Others wore rough dressings, splints and slings;
A few had turbaned heads, the dirty cloth
Brown-badged with blood. A humble
    brotherhood,
Not one was suffering from a lethal hurt,
They were not magnified by noble wounds,
There was no splendour in that company.
And yet, remembering after eighteen years,
In the heart's throat a sour sadness stirs;
Imagination pauses and returns

To see them walking still, but multiplied
In thousands now. And when heroic corpses
Turn slowly in their decorated sleep
And every ambulance has disappeared
The walking wounded still trudge down that lane,
And when recalled they must bear arms again.

*Vernon Scannell*

*from* TO GIVE COMFORT

Days
of torrential rain
relieve us
of the August sun

weeds
and wild flowers
bloom
riotously

at their first
taste of
sweet potato
since the bombing

patients
throughout the ward
murmur
'*Oishii!*'

and I
startle everyone – and myself –
   crying
violently and without shame

for my daughters

*Marc Kaminsky*

# Casualty – Mental Ward

Something has gone wrong inside my head.
The sappers have left mines and wire behind,
I hold long conversations with the dead.

I do not always know what has been said;
The rhythms, not the words, stay in my mind;
Something has gone wrong inside my head.

Not just the sky but grass and trees are red,
The flares and tracers – or I'm colour-blind;
I hold long conversations with the dead.

Their presence comforts and sustains like bread;
When they don't come its hard to be resigned;
Something has gone wrong inside my head.

They know about the snipers that I dread
And how the world is booby-trapped and mined;
I hold long conversations with the dead;

As all eyes close, they gather round my bed
And whisper consolation. When I find
Something has gone wrong inside my head
I hold long conversations with the dead.

*Vernon Scannell*

# LADY IN BLACK

Lady in black,
I knew your son.
Death was our enemy
Death and his gun.

Death had a trench
And he blazed away.
We took that trench
By the end of the day.

Lady in black
Your son was shot.
He was my mate
And he got it hot.

Death's a bastard
Keeps hitting back.
But a war's a war
Lady in black

Birth hurt bad
But you didn't mind.
Well maybe Death
Can be just as kind.

So take it quiet
The same as your son.
Death's only a vicar
Armed with a gun.

And one day Death
Will give it back
And then you can speak to him tidy
Lady in black.

*Alun Lewis*

# KILLED IN ACTION
(For N.J. de B.-L.)

His chair at the table, empty,
His home clothes hanging in rows forlorn,
His cricket bat and cap, his riding cane,
The new flannel suit he had not worn.
His dogs, restless, with tortured ears
Listening for his swift, light tread upon the path.
And there – his violin! Oh his violin! Hush! hold
    your tears.

*Juliette de Bairacli-Levy*
*Crete, May 1941*

# Song of the Dying Gunner

Oh mother my mouth is full of stars
As cartridges in the tray
My blood is a twin-branched scarlet tree
And it runs all runs away.

Oh *Cooks to the Galley* is sounded off
And the lads are down in the mess
But I lie done by the forrard gun
With a bullet in my breast.

Don't send me a parcel at Christmas time
Of socks and nutty and wine
And don't depend on a long weekend
By the Great Western Railway line.

Farewell, Aggie Weston, the Barracks at Guz,
Hang my tiddley suit on the door
I'm sewn up neat in a canvas sheet
And I shan't be home no more.

*Charles Causley*

# WAR LETTERS

The letters are shockingly real,
Like the personal belongings
Of someone recently dead.

The letters are permanent,
And written with our hands,
Which crease into their lines

And breathe, but are not so
Living as these letters
Our hands are seas apart;

A pair might cease to live
While the indestructible letter
Turned lies, flew to the other.

The letters express a love
We cannot realize:
Like a poignant glove

Surviving a well-known hand
They can outlast our bodies
And our love transcend.

*Roy Fuller*

# Simplify Me When I'm Dead

Remember me when I am dead
and simplify me when I'm dead.

As the processes of earth
strip off the colour and the skin
take the brown hair and blue eye

and leave me simpler than at birth,
when hairless I came howling in
as the moon came in the cold sky.

Of my skeleton perhaps
so stripped, a learned man will say
'He was of such a type and intelligence,' no more.

Thus when in a year collapse
particular memories, you may
deduce, from the long pain I bore

the opinions I held, who was my foe
and what I left, even my appearance
but incidents will be no guide.

Time's wrong-way telescope will show
a minute man ten years hence
and by distance simplified.

Through that lens see if I seem
substance or nothing: of the world
deserving mention or charitable oblivion

not by momentary spleen
or love into decision hurled,
leisurely arrive at an opinion.

Remember me when I am dead
and simplify me when I'm dead.

*Keith Douglas*

## Postscript: For Gweno

If I should go away,
Beloved, do not say
'He has forgotten me'.
For you abide,
A singing rib within my dreaming side;
You always stay.
And in the mad tormented valley
Where blood and hunger rally
And Death the wild beast is uncaught, untamed,
Our soul withstands the terror
And has its quiet honour
Among the glittering stars your voices named.

*Alun Lewis*

# THE SENTRY

I have begun to die.
For now at last I know
That there is no escape
From Night. Not any dream
Nor breathless images of sleep
Touch my bat's-eyes. I hang
Leathery-arid from the hidden roof
Of Night, and sleeplessly
I watch within Sleep's province.
I have left
The lovely bodies of the boy and girl
Deep in each other's placid arms;
And I have left
The beautiful lanes of sleep
That barefoot lovers follow to this last
Cold shore of thought I guard.
I have begun to die
And the guns' implacable silence
Is my black interim, my youth and age,
In the flower of fury, the folded poppy,
Night.

*Alun Lewis*

# THE FALLEN

When they fall, men grasp at feathers,
Cheat the knowledge of their doom
With hot hopes, and see all weathers
Fine, not overhung with gloom.

They have failed, and there's no falling
Further. Uncrowned heads are light.
Ambition no more is calling.
Restlessness has passed with fright.

None but fools offer their pity
To the fallen who at last,
Driven from their tyrant city,
Into freedom have been cast.

*John Gawsworth*

# EARLY SPRING

Now that the young buds are tipped with a falling
    sun –
Each twig a candle, a martyr, St Julian's branched
    stag –
And the shadows are walking the cobbled square
    like soldiers
With their long legs creaking and their pointed
    hands
Reaching the railings and fingering the stones
Of what expended, unprojected graves:
The soil's a flirt, the lion Time is tamed,
And pain like a cat will come home to share your
    room.

*Sidney Keyes*

## SONNET: PARTHENOGENESIS

Strange, the unpatterned riot of these years;
A trackless garden bright with ruin, sown
With pale enthusiasms and fed with tears
And flowered of joy, the blossom soonest blown.
I have sought much, pursued the ancient stars
And lusted after spiritual gold;
Drunk colour to the day's end; found in wars
My naked soul drinks deeply, I behold
A finer surge of life. And I have run
And tried to laugh, and fancied I have been
To hell and heaven, journeyed with the sun.
But late I have unlearned all that I've seen
In my wracked garden, and found it growing fair
And everlasting summer biding there.

*James Farrar*
*On leave, Summer 1942*

# ATTIC

We stored some dusty things up there.
It smelt of mothballs and bare wood,
A spaceless jumble place to hide.
All day we crouched below the sun
Too young to feel the utter fear.
We heard them scream and beat with sticks –
Now they were near –

                   a widow's world
Crashed through her glass, old limbless
Porcelain and brass, her table
Torn from her late, careful touching.
We trembled. –

              Someone shouted: 'Halt,
Der Führer will das Treiben nicht!'
And all was quiet. –

                 Then my mother
Cooked some food, and we were waiting
For my father's earth-worn footfall
Returning from the darkening trees.

*Lotte Kramer*

# PEOPLE WEEPING

I was born
in the middle
of a provisional government

allies
willing
to help us

my earliest memories
are of
people weeping

we were
newly arrived prisoners
recently survived victims

we were
women still searching
we were men still hoping

we were
others
who had given up

we were
forgotten lovers
and lost fathers

we were
left-over daughters
and missing mothers

we were
awkward
and uncomfortable

angry
restless guests
in Germany

lists of the dead
and the living
were posted daily

there were
no lists
of those of us

stuck
between
lists.

*Lily Brett*

# I KEEP FORGETTING

I keep forgetting
the facts and statistics
and each time
I need to know them

I look up books
these books line
twelve shelves
in my room

I know where to go
to confirm the fact
that in the Warsaw Ghetto
there were 7.2 people per room

and in Lodz
they allocated
5.8 people
to each room

I forget
over and over again
that one third of Warsaw
was Jewish

and in the ghetto
they crammed 500,000 Jews
into 2.4 per cent
of the area of the city

and how many
bodies were they burning
in Auschwitz
at the peak of their production

twelve thousand a day
I have to check
and re-check

and did I dream
that at 4 p.m. on the 19th January
58,000 emaciated inmates
were marched out of Auschwitz

was I right
to remember that in Bergen Belsen
from the 4th–13th of April 1945
28,000 Jews arrived from other camps

I can remember
hundreds and hundreds
of phone numbers

phone numbers
I haven't phoned
for twenty years
are readily accessible

and I can remember
people's conversations
and what someone's wife
said to someone else's husband

what a good memory
you have,
people tell me.

*Lily Brett*

# Every Month

*The ten-year-old girl*

My house
was close to the place where the bomb fell

My mother
was turned to white bone before
the family altar

Grandfather and I
go to visit her on the sixth of every month

Mother
is now living in the temple at Nakajima

Mother
must be so pleased
to see how big I've gotten

but all I see
is the Memorial Panel quietly standing there
no matter how I try
I can't remember what Mother looks like

*Marc Kaminsky*

# Index of First Lines

# Index of Poets

# ACKNOWLEDGEMENTS

The compiler and publisher wish to thank the following for permission to use copyright material:

**Ackland, Valentine**, '7 October, 1940' and 'Black-out', by permission of the estate of Valentine Ackland; **Anderson, Mary Désirée**, 'Dunkirk', 'The Black-out' and 'Blitz', by permission of her Literary Executor; **Barton, Joan**, 'Newgale Sands 1940' and 'First News Reel: September 1939', by permission of Hull History Archives; **Berridge, Elizabeth**, 'Bombed Church', by permission of David Higham Associates Ltd on behalf of the author; **Brittain, Vera**, 'September, 1939' is included by permission of Mark Bostridge and T.J. Brittain-Catlin, Literary Executors for the Estate of Vera Brittain 1970; **Causley, Charles**, 'Song of the Dying Gunner' from *Collected Poems*, by permission of David Higham Associates Ltd on behalf of the author; **Cornford, Frances**, 'From a Lettter to America on a Visit to Sussex: Spring 1942' and 'Autumn Blitz', by permission of Mr Tom Cornford; **Currey, R. N.**, 'Unseen Fire' from *This Other Planet*, published by Routledge, 1945, and 'Firing with Heavy Guns' from *Collected Poems*, by permission of James Currey; **de Bairacli-Levy, Juliette**, 'Killed in Action', by permission of Raffi Nachshol; **Ewart, Gavin**, 'Sonnet, 1940', by permission of the estate of Gavin Ewart; **Fuller, Roy**, 'Troopship' and 'War Letters' from *Selected Poems*, by permission of Carcanet Press Limited; **Gosling, E. F.**, 'Mechanization', by permission of Jane Glossop; **Jarrell, Randall**, 'Mail Call' and 'A Lullaby', by permission of Faber and Faber on behalf of the author; **Jennings, Elizabeth**, 'The Second World War' from *Collected Poems*, published by Carcanet Press Limited, by permission of David Higham Associates Ltd on behalf of the author; **Kaminsky, Marc**, *from* 'To Give Comfort' and 'Every Month', by permission of the author; **MacNeice, Louis**, 'The Sunlight on the Garden' from *Collected Poems*, Faber and Faber, by permission of David Higham Associates Ltd on behalf of the author; **Pudney,**

**John**, 'Empty Your Pockets' and 'For Johnny' from *For Johnny – Poems of World War II*, Shepheard Walwyn, by permission of David Higham Associates Ltd on behalf of the author; **Read, Herbert**, 'Aeroplanes' from *Selected Poetry*, Sinclair-Stevenson, by permission of David Higham Associates Ltd on behalf of the author; **Reed, Henry**, 'Lessons of the War (To Alan Michell)' from *Collected Poems*, by permission of Carcanet Press Limited; **Scannell, Vernon**, 'War Graves at El Alamein', 'Walking Wounded' and 'Casualty – Mental Ward', by permission of The Estate of Vernon Scannell; **Shand Allfrey, Phyllis**, 'Cunard Liner 1940', by permission of her Literary Executor; **Stevens, Wallace**, 'Martial Cadenza', by permission of Faber and Faber on behalf of the author; **Thwaite, Anthony**, 'Bournemouth, September 3rd, 1939' from *Collected Poems*, Enitharmon Press, 2007, by permission of the author; **Wright, Judith**, 'The Trains' from *Selected Poems*, ETT Imprint, Sydney, 1996, by permission of Mr Tom Thompson.